COUNTRY STORE

— TO —
CORNER MARKET

· NEW YORK ·

RAYMOND BIAL

Credits

The images that appear in this book are published courtesy of the Adirondack Museum, Albany Public Library History Collection; Brooklyn Public Library; Cornwall Public Library; Freeport Historical Society & Museum and Freeport Public Library; the Library of Congress, Prints & Photographs Division; Liverpool Public Library Crawford Collection; McGraw Historical Society; New York Historical Museum (NYHM; New York Public Library (NYPL); Nyack Public Library; Onondaga County Public Library, Local History and Genealogy Department; Patterson Historical Society and Patterson Public Library; Perry Historical Society; Clifton Public Library, Town of Clifton Park History Collection; Voorheesville Public Library Archives. The contributing institutions are indicated with each of the photographs on the following pages.

America Through Time is an imprint of Fonthill Media LLC
www.through-time.com
office@through-time.com

Published by Arcadia Publishing by arrangement with Fonthill Media LLC
For all general information, please contact Arcadia Publishing:
Telephone: 843-853-2070
Fax: 843-853-0044
E-mail: sales@arcadiapublishing.com
For customer service and orders:
Toll-Free 1-888-313-2665

www.arcadiapublishing.com

First published 2021

ISBN 978-1-63499-326-5

Typeset in Mrs Eaves XL Serif Narrow
Printed and bound in England

CONTENTS

About the Author

RAYMOND BIAL (pronounced "beal") has been taking photographs and creating books for nearly fifty years. To date, he has published more than 100 books for children and adults. Raymond's most recent books include *The Shaker Village*, a lovely collection of color photographs depicting the simplicity and grace of this remarkable community. He has also published several works of fiction, including *Chigger*, a touching and humorous novel, and several scary mysteries and collections of ghost stories. Among his most popular books over the years have been *Where Lincoln Walked* and *The Underground Railroad*.

Tribute

This is a bittersweet moment. I'm pleased that this book, the latest fruit of my husband Raymond's labors, has come into the world. At the same time, I'm filled with sadness knowing that this is his last book, one that he worked on right up until the end, when he passed away from heart failure on January 1, 2021. Raymond was endlessly fascinated by history, most especially by the details and minutiae of everyday life that are so often forgotten. Working on this book and its predecessors allowed him to combine several of his most passionate interests: photography, history, and writing. He spent many happy hours immersed in research, finding just the right historical photos to portray his topic, reading about American social history to learn all he could on his subject of interest, and finally distilling all he had learned into brief yet informative captions so that he could share it with his readers.

My family and I are grateful to Fonthill Media and Arcadia Publishing for providing Raymond with the opportunity to do this work that he enjoyed so much and found so rewarding, while capturing the fascinating history of Americans going about their daily lives over the decades, which included shopping for groceries, in photos and text. We miss Raymond terribly, yet are glad to have this book, along with the many others he'd written over the years, to contribute to our cherished store of memories of him.

LINDA BIAL

INTRODUCTION

Country stores and corner markets tend to fascinate anyone who appreciates social and cultural history, and the charm of days gone by. It is no surprise that the lively enterprises, evolving from dry goods stores to general stores, mercantile, and groceries, are at the heart of American life, in both small towns and city neighborhoods. Many of us grew up with these stores, beginning with frequent trips to the local market with parents or grandparents. Or we have heard stories of old times from great grandparents, probably more than once.

The most familiar of everyday places for common people, country stores and city markets have enjoyed a long, colorful, and varied history from the early colonies to the western frontier. This is especially true of New York. There are small towns upstate and then there is "The City," perhaps the most unique in the world. The city and state tell a vivid story of people over centuries, from flinty Yankee farmers to last week's Asian immigrants to Queens.

Through vintage illustrations and photographs, this book recounts the variety and history of lively enterprises in small towns to city neighborhoods. The photographs in *Country Store to Corner Market: New York* are as vibrant as the region and races of the people who have made the city and state their home for generations.

The country store was a gathering place for storekeepers, clerks, townspeople, farmers, and field hands, stocking up on dry goods and groceries. Other stopped by just to visit with friends or pick up their mail. People often sat around the potbelly stove to gossip, play cards, and idle away a rainy day.

Similarly, people in New York, Buffalo, and other large cities visited with friends and neighbors at the corner store as they looked over the fresh vegetables and fruit. New Yorkers came to rely on improvised markets—pushcarts set up curbside on the street. Like the "rolling stores" or "groceries on wheels" of the countryside, pushcarts were ideal in a metropolis of high rents and impoverished immigrants struggling to get by. Over time, pushcarts gathered in open-air markets to sell directly from their vehicle or in stalls. These markets became especially popular in New York and other major cities where fresh fish and farm produce were brought in every day. Some markets came to be set indoors or at least with a roof against the whims of weather.

Town or country, early dry goods stores carried items that kept well. These included coffee, flour, sugar, crackers, spices, pickles, vinegar, and molasses that people could not make for themselves. Storekeepers lined their shelves from floor to ceiling and piled the counter with these staples, and perhaps a jar of penny candy on the counter. Dry goods were stacked in the middle of the floor; stored in barrels, boxes, and bins; and hung on hooks from the tin ceiling. All these items were stocked in bulk. The storekeeper measured or weighed the desired amount and poured it into bags for customers. Dry goods stores evolved into general stores that also stocked tinned foods such as sardines, oysters, peaches, and other "fancy groceries." Families had no refrigeration other than an icebox, so housewives had to shop for fresh meat and vegetables every day or two. General stores also stocked or could backorder everything from bolts of cloth to farm equipment. They often housed the local post office. They sold merchandise for "cash money," offered credit to customers against a factory paycheck or a farm harvest, or rural folks traded for fresh eggs, butter, vegetables, and fruit. In the city, people paid cash or credit, if the customer was known in the neighborhood.

Most importantly, people had to walk to the store located near their home. It was convenient if there was a subway stop or streetcar line nearby and the stores and pushcart markets were all situated within walking distance of their shoppers' homes. Gatherings of pushcarts and corner markets each attracted several hundred regular customers. Like their country cousins, city stores flourished from the late nineteenth into the twentieth centuries. Many stores reflected the immigrant culture of the neighborhood—Italian, Jewish, Chinese, and many others. These grocers carried foods from the "old country" and did business in the native language of their customers. By the early years of the twentieth century, small groceries dotted every city neighborhood and every small town in the state.

The rise of chain stores, notably the Great Atlantic and Pacific Tea Company (A&P) and Kroger, threatened mom-and-pop groceries—and a way of life. People could now drive a new invention—the automobile—to supermarkets beyond their neighborhood. These chain stores bought large quantities of products at low prices, often directly from wholesalers or even manufacturers.

Grocery stores called "super markets" remained full-service. A clerk fetched and packaged the items requested by a shopper. However, on September 9, 1916, Clarence Saunders opened a Piggly Wiggly grocery in Memphis, Tennessee, which was the first "self-serving store." Shoppers entered this modern store through turnstiles and strolled down narrow aisles through a maze of shelves stacked with groceries. They selected their items and made their way back to the cashiers at the front of the store, who replaced full-service clerks. The Piggly Wiggly concept grew rapidly through the Great Depression. By the late 1930s, there were over 2,600 self-service groceries nationwide, including in New York. In the city people still relied on public transportation and walked just about everywhere else. Some chains, like A & P and IGA, adapted and opened small stores that have become neighborhood fixtures.

This book is a visual sampler of early stores and markets in the city and state. Laid out chronologically, with captions, the images reveal the strength, good cheer, and occasional heartbreak of people making lives for themselves, their families, and neighbors. I hope that you enjoy *Country Store to Corner Market: New York* as much as I loved looking through thousands of photographs of the generations of people who came before us.

1
COLONIAL NEW YORK IN THE 1800s

This lovely print depicts in an early grocery and genteel tea store on the corner of Spring & Crosby Streets in New York City in 1826. The image appeared in *Booth's History of New York* volume 8, 1828-1890. [*NYPL*]

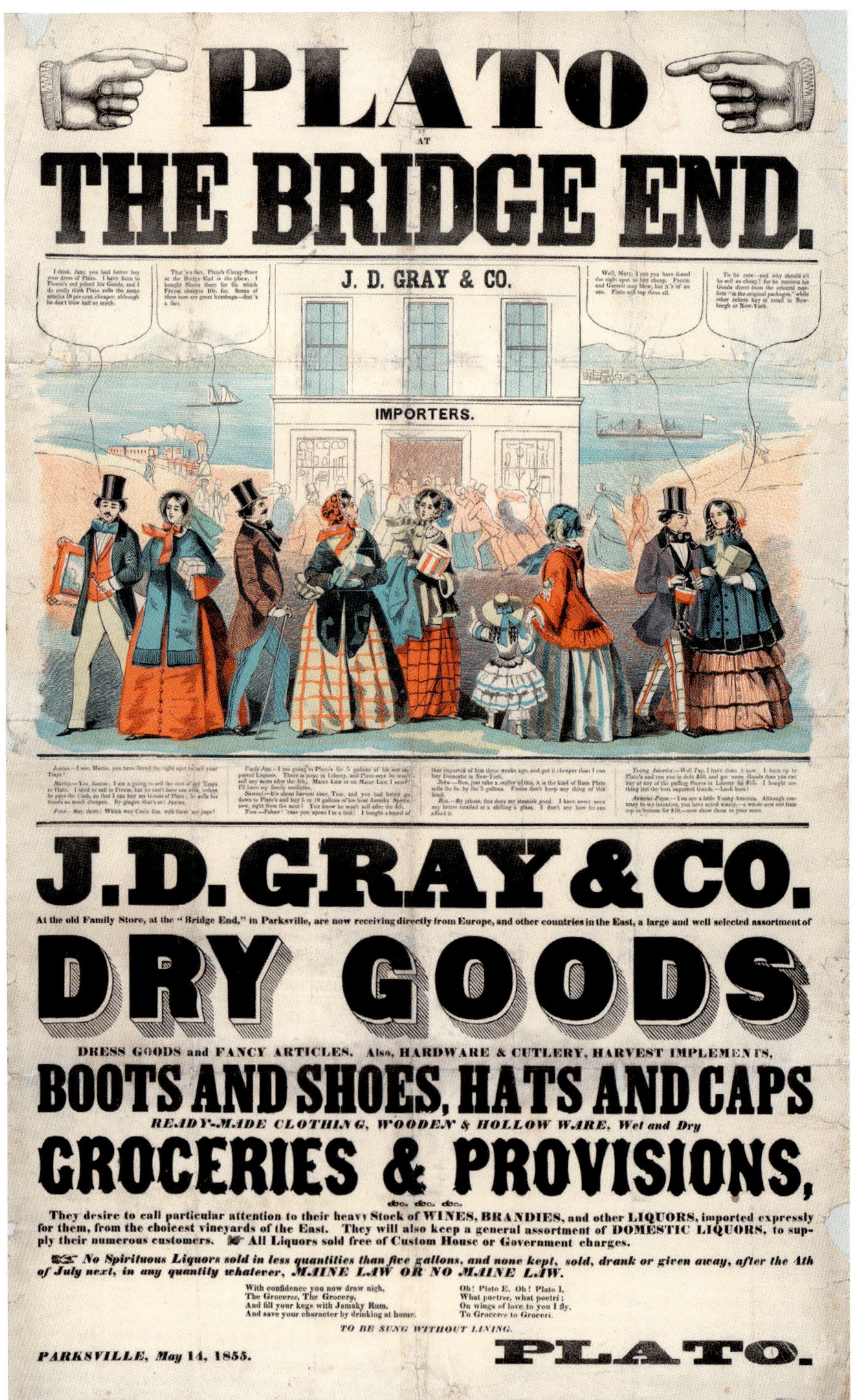

Published on May 14, 1855, this print features a colorful advertisement with fashionable men and women outside James D. Gray & Co. Importers with purchases, as others rush to enter the store. [*Library of Congress*]

This trading card was used by Valentine, Bergen, & Co. Wholesale Grocers" to advertise their business and the soothing qualities of "Alden Fruit Vinegar." In the illustration a woman in blue dress with a bright sun and flowers admits, "I am soulfully intense." [*Brooklyn Public Library*]

Artist A. B. (Arthur Burdett) Frost (1851-1928) made the fine sketch and Lagarde made the engraving of a meat store at Fulton Market. Written on the border of the print are "Jan 5, 1878, the Christmas season," and "game stand." [*NYPL*]

2
UPSTATE NEW YORK

Four men—probably the Doersch Brothers—pose in front of the Wigwam general store in Nyack, New York, in 1880. The town hall once stood here. The book *Old Nyack* stated, "Horace Greeley spoke here ... town events centered here in the old hall when Grant was President." [*Nyack Public Library*]

Here is a stereoscopic view of H. Hager grocery store, which did business in Central New York in the late 1800s, probably around 1870-1890. The albumen print depicts the owner and able employees in front with an array of dry goods in barrels and baskets. [*NYPL*]

Henry Tucker operated Tucker, Kent & Co. Store on Front Street in Patterson, New York. Noted on photo: "Taken a few years after 1888 when my father came over from Sweden." (Claus) C. A. Moline is on the right and Mr. Tucker is second from the left. Hilda (Moline) Dahm-man is on his right. [*Patterson Historical Society and Patterson Public Library*]

This postcard depicts a two-story grocery store with wraparound porch in Freeport, New York, at the turn of the century. A horse-drawn wagon identified as "Heide's, Sold Everywhere," stands out front and the store sign reads: "R.H. Mollineaux, Groceries Flour & Feed." [*Freeport Historical Society & Museum and Freeport Public Library*]

Opposite page:

Above: This early postcard features Osborne's Chester Market, which William Osborne operated around the turn of the century. The popular store was located in downtown Chester (Village), Orange County, New York.

Below: Here is a newspaper advertisement for Osborne's Chester Market and accountant C. H. Fredericks. The local market was operated by William Osborne in the village of Chester, New York. The ad was published in the June 6, 1898, of the *Weekly News*.

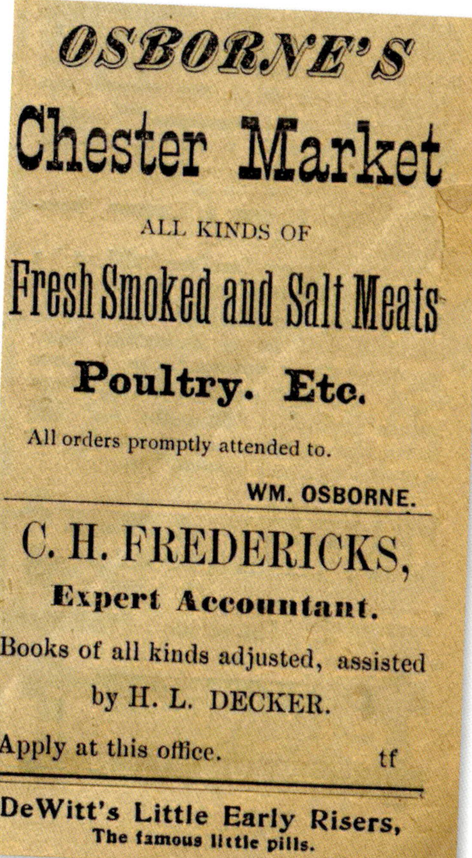

OSBORNE'S
Chester Market

ALL KINDS OF

Fresh Smoked and Salt Meats
Poultry. Etc.

All orders promptly attended to.

WM. OSBORNE.

C. H. FREDERICKS,
Expert Accountant.

Books of all kinds adjusted, assisted
by H. L. DECKER.

Apply at this office.   tf

DeWitt's Little Early Risers,
The famous little pills.

3

UPSTATE:
TURN OF THE CENTURY TO 1930

The dignified proprietors and clerks, possibly their wives, posed for this photograph in front of the Watkins and McKurth Grocery in Perry, New York, in 1908. The women and men are understandably proud of the enterprise they have built over the years. [*Perry Public Library*]

The Watkins and McKurth Grocery was located in the small town of Perry on North Main Street. Left to right are Emma Nevins, Mabel Beardsley (later Mrs. Robert Hall), Frank McKurth, and Floyd Smith. Watkins and McKurth sold the grocery prior to 1915. [*Perry Public Library*]

Taken between 1895 and 1910 by Detroit Publishing Company, this photograph depicts the barroom and grocery of Charles W. Seymour in Plattsburg, New York. The ornate cash register is perhaps the most prominent feature in this establishment. [*Library of Congress*]

This photograph by Bain News Service shows how children cooled off on a hot day. On July 6, 1912, the youngsters had fun licking a large block of ice on the sidewalk in front of a grocery store in Buffalo, New York. [*Library of Congress*]

Klein's Cash Grocery (misspelled Cach) was established in 1835 by Nathan Clark and purchased by Samuel Klein in 1914. Cornwall Landing was one of the busiest harbors on the Hudson River from the early 1700s until the 1960s. [*Cornwall Public Library*]

Established in 1835 by Nathan Clark and purchased by Samuel Klein in 1914, this image shows the well-stocked interior of Klein's Cash Grocery and General Store. It was located on Cornwall Landing, a busy harbor on the Hudson River. [*Cornwall Public Library*]

In 1922, display cases and shelves were crammed with canned and boxed foods in the Trading Port store in Albany. The owner, Abraham Tabachneck, "Pop," is seated behind the stove. Isadore Tabachneck, "Izzy," is standing behind the counter. [*Albany Public Library History Collection*]

Opposite page:

Above: Several people in the Patterson Meat Market in Patterson, New York, hammed it up for the camera in this photograph taken about 1925. They are, left to right: George Pfahl, Lester Pfahl, Fannie Sprague, Mildred Johnson, and George Colvin (standing in back). [*Patterson Historical Society and Patterson Public Library*]

Below: Julia and Jamilia Ossite with their mother, Mariam Ossite, stand in the doorway of Wilson Ossite Grocery, McGraw, New York. There are Durkee's bread and SPUD cigarettes advertisements and gas pumps. [*McGraw Historical Society*]

A.W. OSSITE CASH GROCERY.

"SALADA" TEA

Durkee's FUL·MILK BREAD

ALL THE VITAMINS OF MILK & BUTTER

SALADA TEA

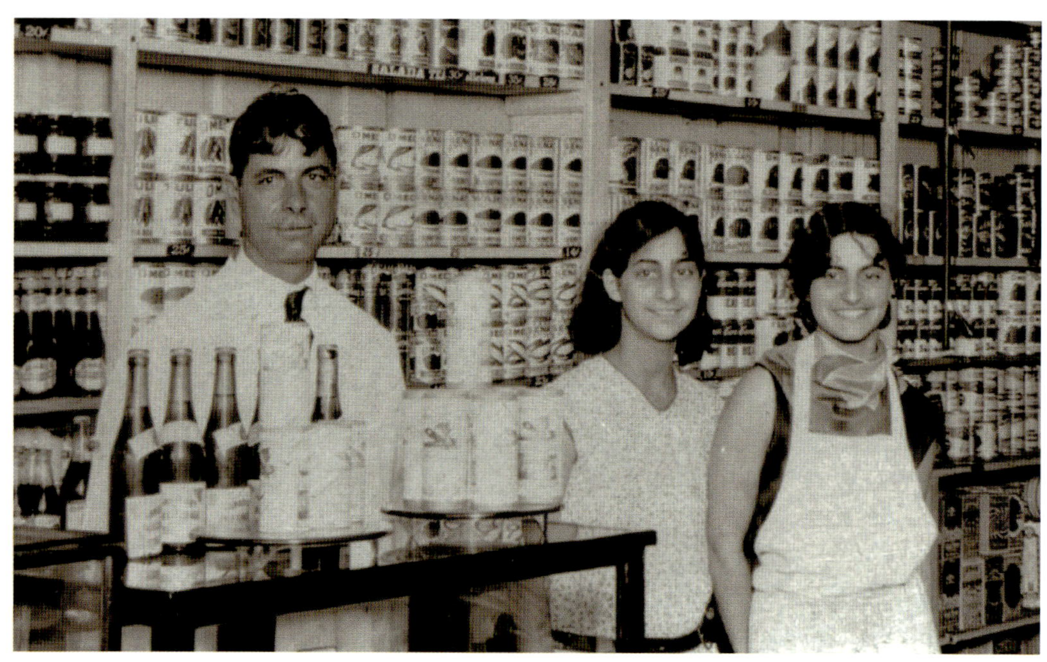

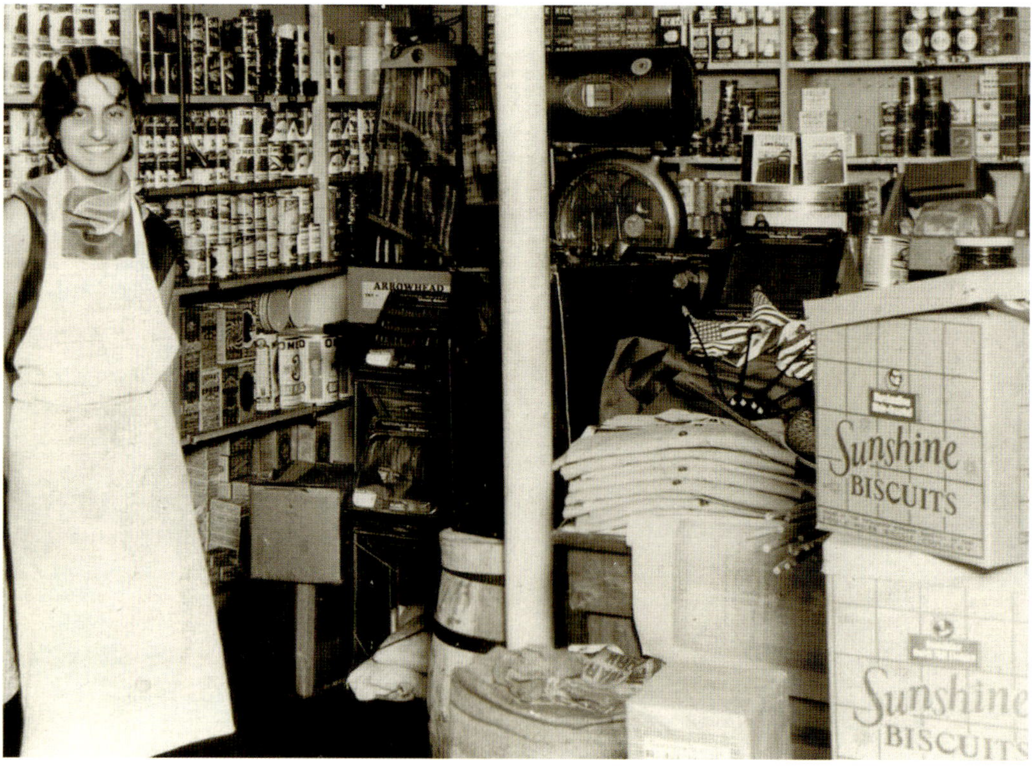
ARROWHEAD
Sunshine
BISCUITS
Sunshine
BISCUITS

A. Traverson Fruits and Vegetables was located in Nyack, New York. About 1930, a delivery truck parked in front of the store, where vegetables were displayed in crates and bushel baskets. A man sat behind the steering wheel and a woman stood in the doorway. [*Nyack Public Library*]

Opposite page:

Above: This Italian-American family (Jasper, Antonetta, and Josephine Tork) owned and operated the Arrowhead grocery in Voorheesville, New York. Taken about 1925-30, the portrait includes shelves of canned goods behind them. [*Voorheesville Public Library Archives*]

Below: About 1925-1930, Josephine Tork posed for this portrait in her Italian-American family's grocery, known as the Arrowhead Store in Voorheesville, New York. She was listed as a sales lady and the daughter of Jasper Tork, the owner of the store. [*Voorheesville Public Library*]

About 1930-1935, owners Gerald and Gifford Caldwell posed for this photograph in the Victory Chain grocery store in McGraw, Cortland County, New York. The two men are standing in midst of counters and shelves of canned goods and other groceries. [*McGraw Historical Society*]

This photograph depicts the I. Davis Aqueduct Grocery store on Aqueduct Road in Niskayuna, Schenectady County, New York, in the 1930s. The store is adorned with signs for Coca-Cola, Sealtest ice cream, Salada tea, and Camel cigarettes. [*Nyack Public Library*]

4
UPSTATE:
GREAT DEPRESSION AND WAR

This ornate potbelly stove, also known as a Franklin stove, stood prominently in a general store in the small town of Wilson, Niagara County, New York. The photograph of the old stove warming the store was taken in November 1941. [*Library of Congress*]

Photographed by Jack Delano, this country store and post office was located in the village of Sterlingville, New York. The country store had to be demolished to make room for an expansion of Pine Camp at the onset of World War II. [*Library of Congress*]

Above left: Photographed by Marjory Collins in May 1943, Beverly Ann Grimm, eleven, purchased groceries at a small store in Buffalo, New York, on a list her mother left for her. Her twenty-six-year-old mother was widowed and now busy working on the home front. [*Library of Congress*]

Above right: Photographed by Marjory Collins in May 1943, Peter Grimm, aged ten, waits with his wagon outside Loblaw's grocery store on a rainy day. Peter can make enough deliveries to help out his young mother, a working widow. Most likely the husband and father died early in the war. [*Library of Congress*]

5

UPSTATE:
FAMILIAR TOWNS AND STREETS

Taken about 1948, George Hayden is standing in front of the Hayden grocery store at 808 McBride Street in Syracuse, New York. His family moved to Syracuse from Bamberg, South Carolina, in the 1930s. [*Onondaga County Public Library*]

This photograph by Joe Wentworth depicts Heid's Grocery Store, 209 Oswego Street, Liverpool, New York, about 1950. Val Heid is standing in front of his store and his delivery van. [*Liverpool Public Library*]

Opposite page:

Above: Burl Smith and George Pfahl pose in front of Patterson Market in 1938, as evidenced by the Armour Star Ham advertisement in the window. Armour used the popularity of the new Disney film *Snow White and the Seven Dwarfs* to promote their Easter ham in 1938. [*Patterson Historical Society and Patterson Public Library*]

Below: Knapp's Superette (IGA Stores) was located on Front Street, Patterson, New York. The small grocery opened as a First National Store around 1930. In 1953, it became Knapp's Superette, named after the owners Jesse and Mildred Knapp. Mrs. Knapp can be seen in the left-hand window. [*Patterson Historical Society and Patterson Public Library*]

TTERSON MARKET
ETABLES · FISH · PROVISIONS

KNAPP'S SUPERETTE
I.G.A. STORES
IGA
IGA
Marlene
MARGARINE
22
MAYONNAISE
39

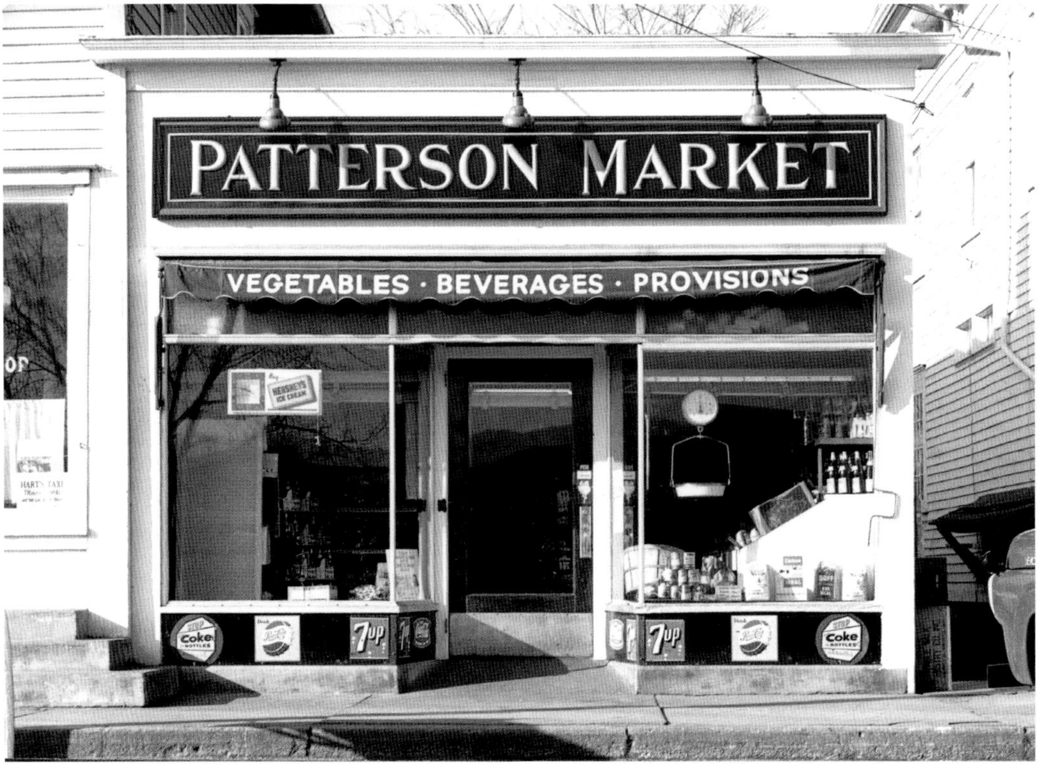

By SUPPORTING
FRI. JULY 17
At 10 A.M.
SPONSORED BY TH
(Brooklyn Terminal
WALDBAUM WILL
CANARSIE WATER

This portrait of the Bonadonne family was taken inside Bonadonne's Market in Perry, Wyoming County, New York, probably between 1970 and 1979. Many small groceries were family owned and operated. Shown here is Sam, father, and sons, Nick and Joey. [*Perry Public Library*]

Opposite page:

Above: Brothers George and Lester Pfahl managed the Patterson Market when this photograph was taken about 1960. For more than a century from about the 1860s to the 1960s, the little store served as a popular meat market on Front Street in Patterson, Putnam County, New York. [*Patterson Historical Society and Patterson Public Library*]

Below: Martin Krichmar of Waldbaum Supermarkets hands a large slice of watermelon to John Friscia, age four, while other children look on, hoping he'll share some. Phyllis Twachtman documented this event in this photograph for the *New York World-Telegram and the Sun Newspaper* in 1964. [*Library of Congress*]

In 1986-1987, Mathias T. Oppersdorff photographed Emanuel Maroun and a young woman outside Maroun's Market in Tupper Lake, New York. It is a fine portrait and wistful look at the loss of stores in small towns. [*Adirondack Museum*]

In 1986-1987, Mathias T. Oppersdorff photographed Emanuel Maroun Emanuel Maroun standing outside Maroun's Market in Tupper Lake, New York. It is a rare glimpse at small stores disappearing from the New York countryside. [*Adirondack Museum*]

6

NEW YORK CITY

New York City kids have always known how to have fun, hopping a subway car at Coney Island, riding the goat carriages there (1904), playing stickball in the street, or scrounging up a few pennies for candy at the neighborhood grocery. [*Library of Congress*]

Photographed by Alice Austen in 1896, an immigrant and a pretzel vendor were faces of New York city streets through the nineteenth century. After arriving in "the New Country," people struggled to make a living in small markets or pushcarts on the street. [*Library of Congress*]

Taken for the Detroit Publishing Company between 1890 and 1901, this photograph depicts the Jewish market on the East Side in New York City. The street is crowded with vendors and pushcarts along with shoppers looking for fresh groceries. [*Library of Congress*]

This early color postcard shows a new Jewish market in the Lower East Side in New York City street crowded with pushcart vendors and pedestrians. The photograph was taken for the Detroit Publishing Company between 1901 and 1907. [*Library of Congress*]

This early color photograph shows the bustling market along Mulberry Street in the Lower East Side of New York, about 1900. Taken for the Detroit Publishing Company, the Photochrom color image shows a street crowded with pushcarts and pedestrians. [*Library of Congress*]

BICYCLES
P. AVALLONE

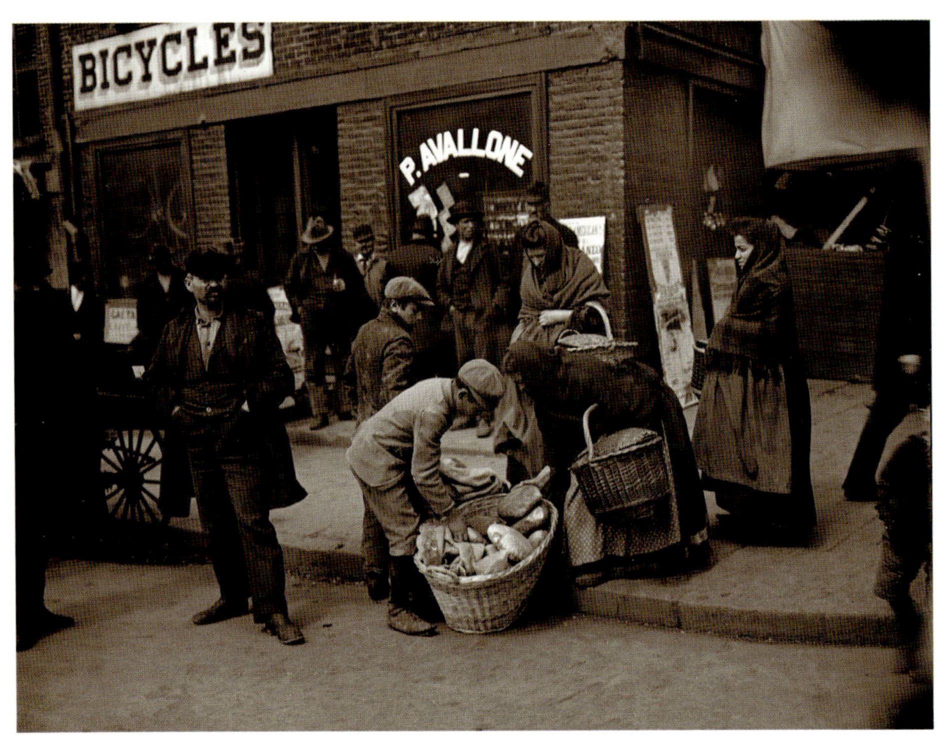

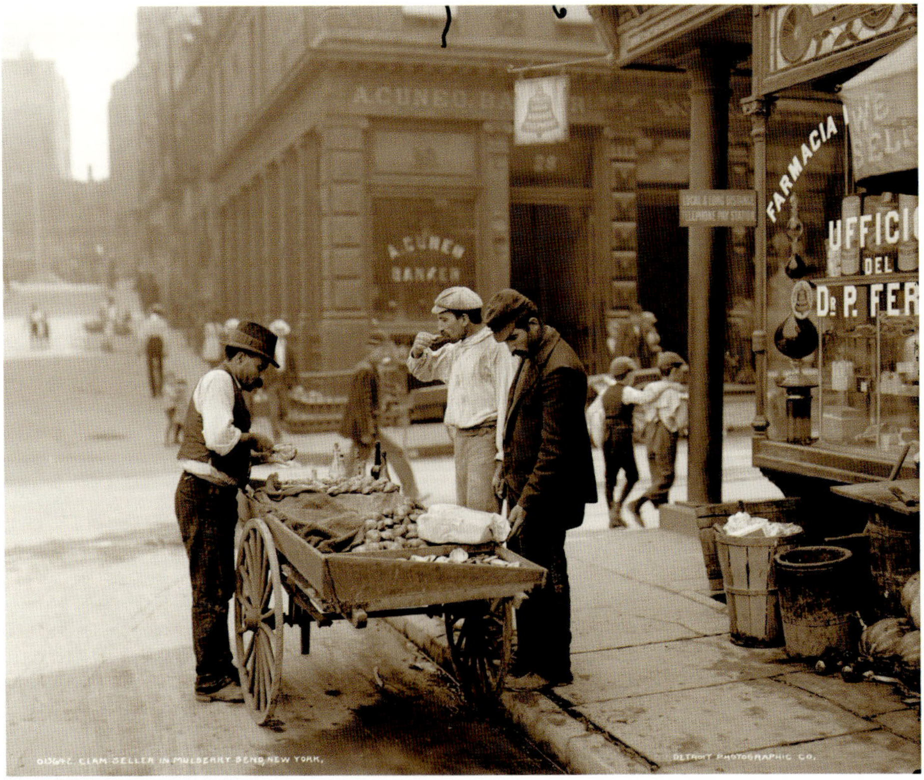
FARMACIA
UFFICIO
DEL
Dr P. FER
CLAM SELLER IN MULBERRY BEND, NEW YORK.
DETROIT PHOTOGRAPHIC CO.

A grocery and delicatessen occupied the ground floor in a tenement house in New York City about 1900 in this photograph for the Detroit Publishing Company. The "Wm. Inwood, groceries" is lettered on the front window on building. [*Library of Congress*]

Opposite page:

Above: This photograph taken for the Detroit Publishing Company depicts several Italian bakers peddling fresh loaves of bread in baskets. They are working at the curb on Mulberry Street in Lower East Side of New York City about 1900. [*Library of Congress*]

Below: Taken about 1900 for the Detroit Publishing Company, this photograph shows a peddler with his pushcart filled with delectable clams. He has set up shop on Mulberry Bend on the Lower East Side of New York City. [*Library of Congress*]

About 1902, George Ehler Stonebridge took this photograph of a stylish delivery cart parked in front of M. & C. Uhly Delicatessen in the Bronx. Delis often conveniently offered grocery items and apparently made deliveries. [Library of Congress]

Opposite page:

Above: Taken in the early 1900s, this photograph shows a child, a pushcart, and an Indian-American grocery in a tenement house, most likely in the East Side. The store carried a variety of goods, including coal in the winter and ice for chilling food in the summer. [*NYPL*]

Below: Published by Underwood & Underwood about 1900-1910, this stereograph captures the bustle of Fulton Market fish dealers, looking north along South Street in New York City. At the time, this was the place to find fresh fish at reasonable prices. [*Library of Congress*]

<h1 style="text-align:center">7</h1>

WALLABOUT MARKET

Horse-drawn wagons gathered in the sprawling Wallabout Market in Brooklyn, New York. This scene is captured in color for a postcard from the turn of the century. The background is the Brooklyn Bridge, which opened in 1883. [*National Archives*]

Opposite page:

Above: This look into the interior of Wallabout Market reveals an abundance of wholesale goods for F. Mosca, Inc. There are boxes, bins, and shelves of canned goods and glass jars of everything from olives to pickles. The precise date of the photograph in not known. [*National Archives*]

Below: This photograph depicts the Wallabout Market in Brooklyn about 1905. At the time, the sprawling market was the second largest food wholesaler in the world. It supplied groceries and pushcarts throughout the city. [*Library of Congress*].

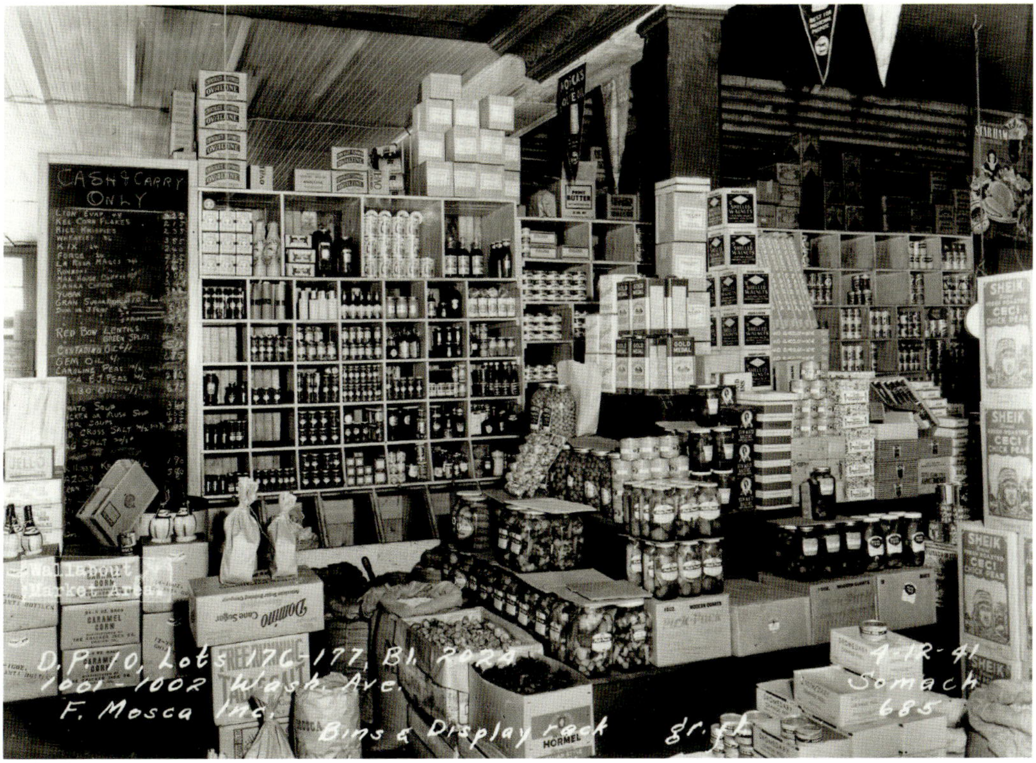

CASH & CARRY ONLY
Wallabout Market Area
D.P. 10, Lots 176-177, Bl. 2023
1001-1002 Wash. Ave.
F. Mosca Inc.
Bins & Display Rack
4-12-41
Somach
685

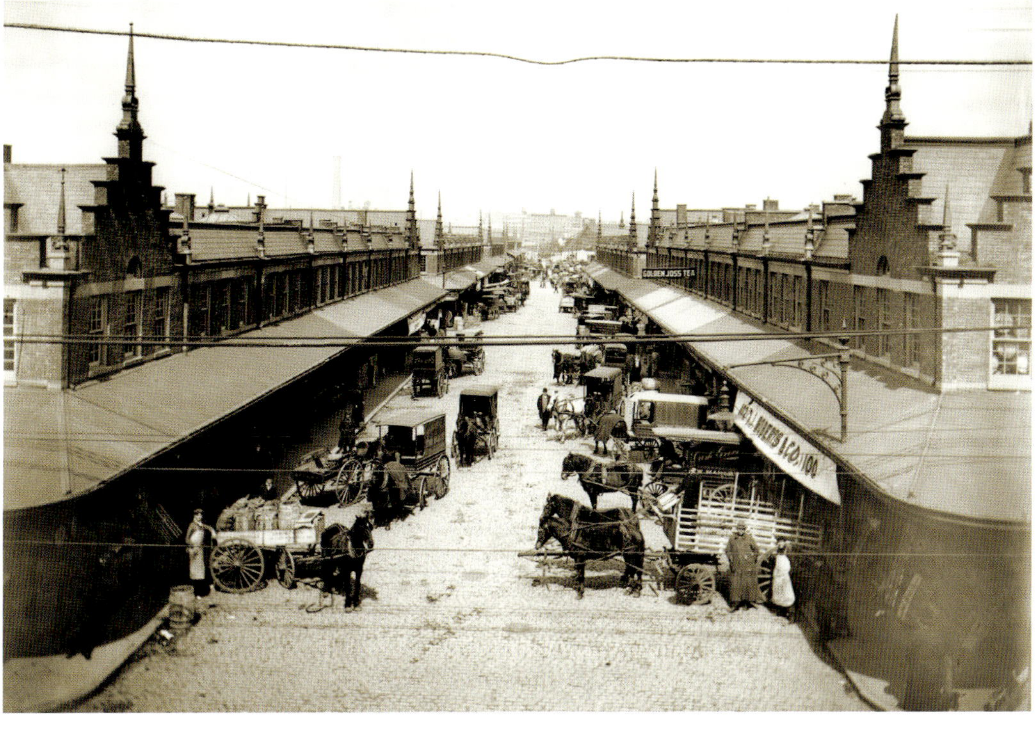

GOLDEN JOSS TEA

Al Aumuller captured the sprawl of Wallabout Market in Brooklyn in this 1940 photograph for the *New York World-Telegram and Sun Newspaper.* The trucks and horse-drawn wagons delivered produce and fish to groceries and pushcart vendors throughout the city. [*Library of Congress*]

8
NYC:
TURN OF THE CENTURY TO 1930

Hungry customers gather around a cluster of lunch carts in this 1906 photograph for the Detroit Publishing Company in 1906. Tended by vendors on Broad Street in New York City, the carts offered a wide range of groceries from peanuts to fresh produce and fish. [*Library of Congress*]

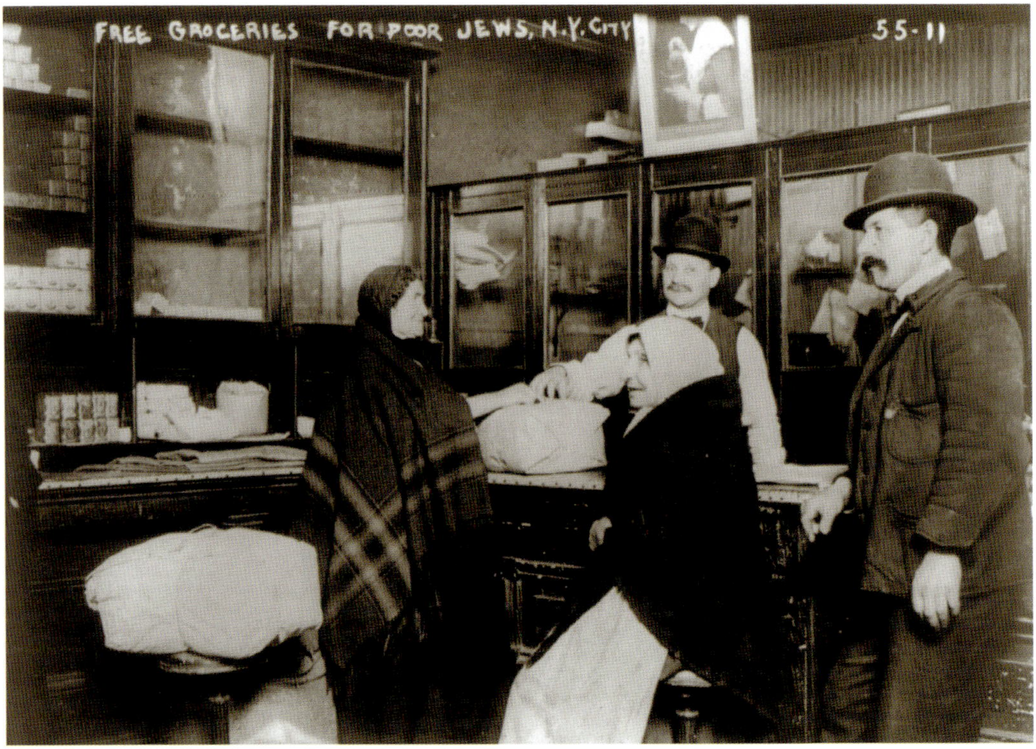

FREE GROCERIES FOR POOR JEWS, N.Y. CITY
55-11

80-2
STREET VENDER, ITALIAN FEAST

Taken for the Detroit Publishing Company between 1900 and 1910, this photograph shows an Italian market on Mulberry Street in New York City. Two women are discussing the bananas and other produce on a stand set up in front of the market. [*Library of Congress*]

Opposite page:

Above: Free groceries were given to poor Jews in New York City in this touching image from 1908. In this photograph taken for Bain News Service, Jewish women and men are gratefully accepting groceries given to them in a neighborhood market. [*Library of Congress*]

Below: Living in a city on the go, New Yorkers often picked up groceries at pushcarts on the way to and from work. In this 1908 photograph from Bain News Service, two street venders offered an "Italian feast" of grapes, dried fruit, and nuts on their pushcart. [*Library of Congress*]

Around 1910, Frank M. Ingalls photographed this Italian woman with a bundle on her head. She is standing by her cart talking with some customers at the pushcart market, 34 Mulberry Street, New York City. [*NYHM*]

This photograph of Rivington Street in New York City was made about 1910 for Bain News Service. It shows a bustling street and sidewalk of lively peddlers and pedestrians looking for bargains. [*Library of Congress*]

This enterprising boy is collecting discarded newspapers in Union Square in New York City. He sells them to storekeepers who in turn re-sell the secondhand newspapers in their stores. Lewis Wickes Hine took this photograph in July 1910. [*Library of Congress*]

Opposite page:

Above: A group of children are sitting on an empty pushcart on the Lower East Side, New York City, about 1910. Most likely it is late in the day after the grocer has sold all the vegetables and fruit on the pushcart. [*Library of Congress*]

Taken for Bain News Service between 1910 and 1915, this photograph shows children paying two cents each for a cruise around the block in a car. In those days two cents bought a lot of candy at the corner store. But automobiles were a novelty, and a joy ride was irresistible. [*Library of Congress*]

AROUND THE BLOCK FOR 2 cents
A FULL LINE OF
SUIT CASES & BAGS
ENTRANCE AROUND THE CORNER

A. SILZ,
POULTRY & GAME.
POULTRY & GAME.

BIG 4
CANDY CO.
BIG FOUR CANDY CO. INC.
4
WHOLESALE CONFECTIONERS.
608 E ST. N.W.
SCHRAFFT'S
CHOCOLATES

William Davis Hassler took this photograph of Creighton's butcher shop and Irving Variety Market in New York City between 1911 and 1921. The proprietor is standing in the shade by the store which also did brisk business in oysters, clams, and fish. [*NYPL*]

Opposite page:

Above: William D. Hassler took this photograph of a delivery wagon for A. Silz Poultry and Game in New York City about 1910-1911. He and other drivers kept the grocers stocked with fresh meat. [*Library of Congress*]

Below: This photograph shows a Semmes truck in front of the Big Four Candy Company that delivered wholesale candy to stores and markets between 1910 and 1926—until Semmes Motor Company was acquired by Mack Trucks. [*Library of Congress*]

ER BROS.
& GROCERIES

MUNGER BROS

VOTES
FOR WOMEN

TROLLEY
CAMPAIGN

This Bain News Service photograph shows how the Pushcart Market on the East Side appeared around 1915. Crowded in a roofed building that provided shelter from the whims of weather, the pushcarts sold an abundance of fruit, vegetables, fish, and meat. [*Library of Congress*]

Opposite page:

Above: Jimmie Chinquanana lived in a dark room in the rear of the family's grocery on Hamilton Street. He was the ninth child, six of whom died. His father drank and beat Jimmie. Lewis W. Hine made this touching photograph on September 16, 1913. [*Library of Congress*]

Below: About 1915 this suffragist asked a grocer if he would place a sign in his store window: "Votes for Women, Trolley Campaign." She also asked if he would put a copy in packages of groceries." The amendment was finally passed by Congress in 1919 and ratified by states in 1920. [*Library of Congress*]

This photograph taken for Bain News Service on June 5, 1917, shows a line of men next to Bahnsen & Roeloffs grocery store in New York City. The men are waiting to register for the draft during World War I, while a policeman is on duty to keep things in order. [*Library of Congress*]

Opposite page:

Above: Photographed by Lewis Wickes Hine for National Child Labor Committee about 1915, this thirteen-year-old Italian boy worked after school behind a grocery counter. He is dressed formally and has a professional air about him. [*Library of Congress*]

Below: On the Lower East Side of New York City, this Italian immigrant is peddling bread on the streets in 1916. In the photograph taken for Bain News Service, the woman appears to be especially proud of the warm loaves that have just come out of the bakery oven. [*Library of Congress*]

This photograph shows men holding draft cards as they come out of a registration station next to Bahnsen & Roeloffs grocery store New York City. The men have just registered for the draft during World War I on June 5, 1917. They are in high spirits, at least for that moment in history. [*Library of Congress*]

Opposite page:

Above: Pushcart vendors were busy at Orchard Street and East Houston Street on September 18, 1929, just before the Stock Market Crash. This photo captured glimpses of everyday street life on New York City. [*NYHM*]

Below: This James Butler Groceries store was located on the northwest corner of Main Street & Irma Avenue, opposite the railroad station in New York City. Taken about 1929, this photograph shows parked cars and people gathered on the sidewalk in front of the grocery. [*NYPL*]

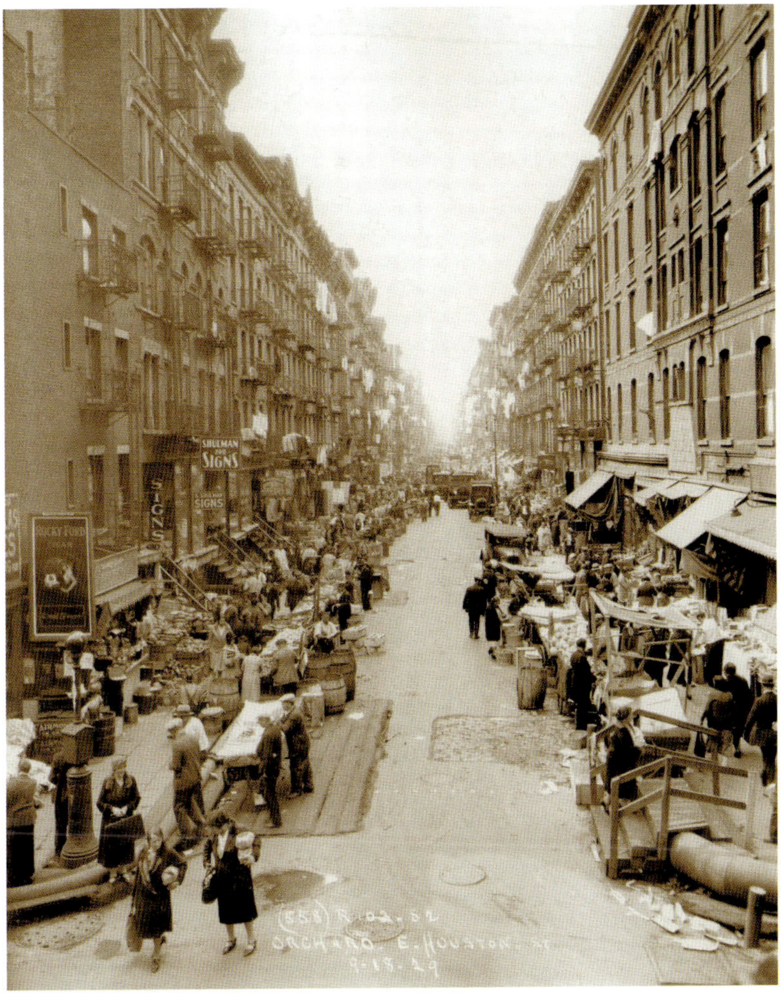
SHULMAN
SIGNS
SIGNS
ORCHARD. E. HOUSTON ST

MEYER RAFF
JAMES BUTLE
GROCERIES

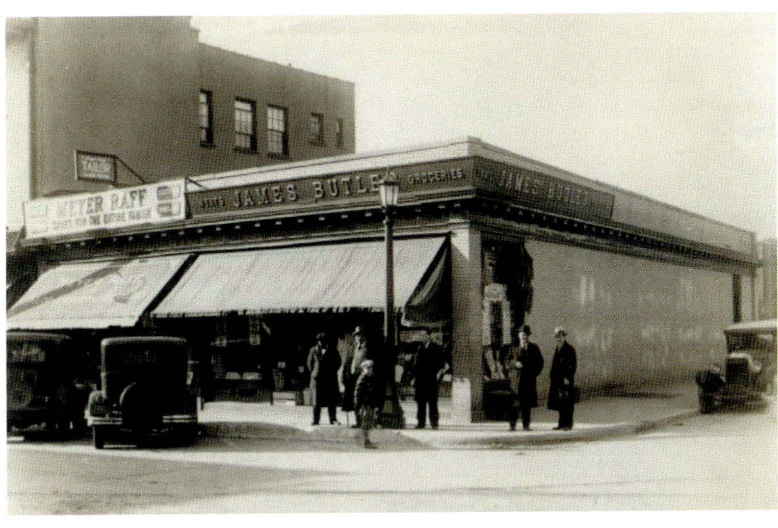

9
NYC:
GREAT DEPRESSION AND WORLD WAR II

This storefront at 29 Washington, New York County, New York, was photographed 1933 for the Historic American Buildings Survey. The window identifies the enterprise as a Greek grocery like many other small ethnic markets in metropolitan New York. [*Library of Congress*]

Noted photographer Berenice Abbott took this storefront image for a Federal Art Project for a collection called "Changing New York" on February 2, 1937. The Italian market was located at 276 Bleecker Street, Manhattan, in Greenwich Village. [*Library of Congress*]

Welton Market relied on this sturdy General Motors truck (Model T 14 B-D16) to deliver wholesale groceries to their store in New York City. On the right in this photograph from May 8, 1937, is a Piggly Wiggly, one of the most innovative and popular stores of the day. [*NYPL*]

Opposite page:

Above: Photographed for the New York (N.Y.). Tenement House Department in 1937, this apartment house and storefronts, notably J.H. Bunger Groceries, was located at 226-230 Fort Washington Avenue-W and 169th Street, in Manhattan. [*NYPL*]

Below: This photograph by inspectors of the New York City Tenement House Department depicts a three-story house with a grocery and meat market on the ground floor in 1938. The neighborhood grocery makes itself known on the large *Coca Cola* sign out front. [*NYPL*]

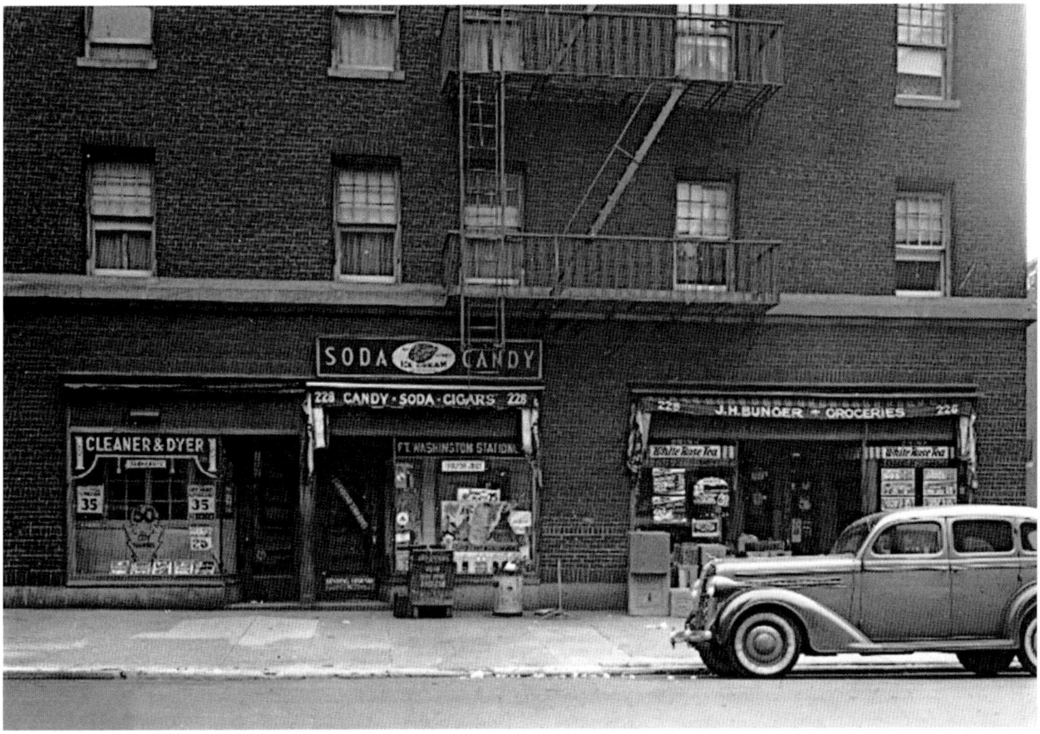
SODA CANDY
228 CANDY - SODA - CIGARS 228
CLEANER & DYER
35
35
228 J.H.BUNGER GROCERIES 228
White Rose Tea
White Rose Tea

Coca-Cola

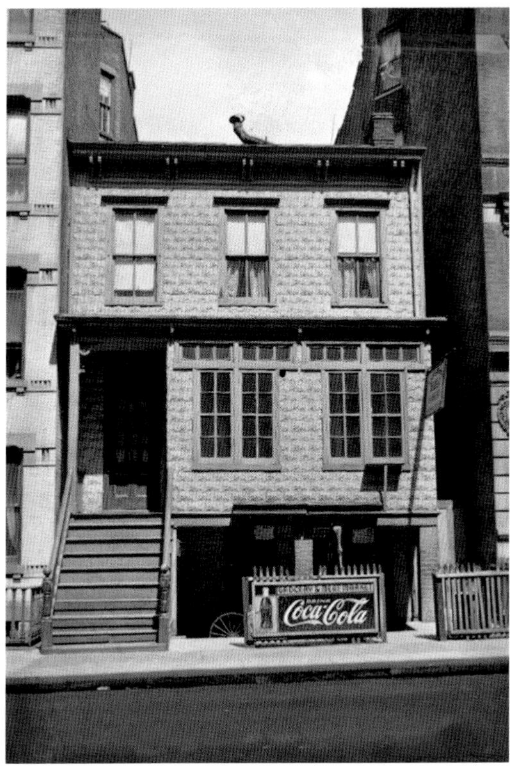

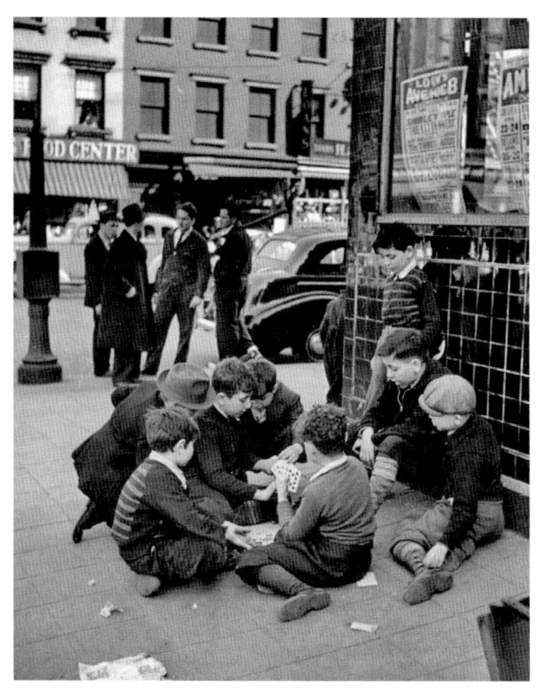

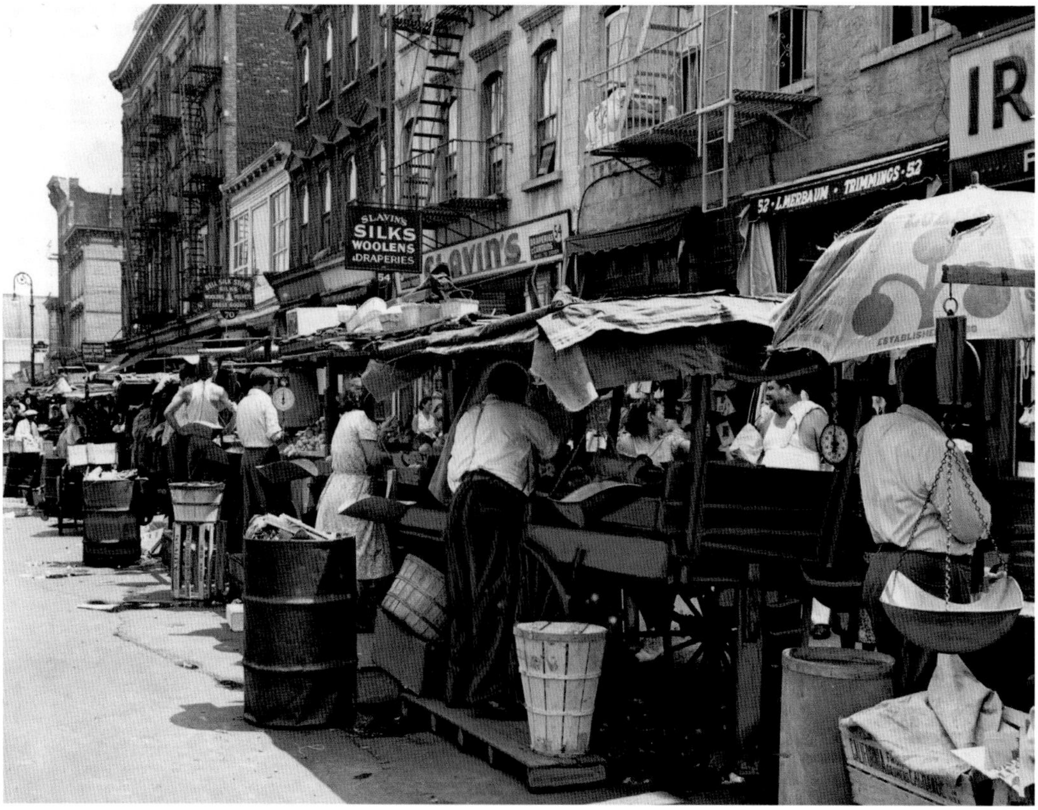
SLAVIN'S
SILKS
WOOLENS
&DRAPERIES
54
SLAVIN'S
52 · L. MERBAUM · TRIMMINGS · 52

Sid Grossman photographed this street scene of a labor union supporter picketing the Lenox Fruit & Vegetable Market in 1939. People passed by the picketer on the sidewalk in front of the boycotted grocery store in Harlem, New York City. [*NYHM*]

Opposite page:

Above: Alexander Alland photographed these young card sharps intensely involved in their game on the sidewalk by a corner market on the Lower East Side. The photograph was taken about 1938, but the boys appeared to be regulars on the sidewalk here. [*NYPL*]

Below: Every vendor appears to be enjoying brisk trade in 1939 when Alan Fisher took photograph for an article in the *New York World-Telegram and Sun Newspaper*. The pushcarts were parked along the curb at the Brownsville, Belmont Avenue market. [*Library of Congress*]

ASSOCIATED
FOOD STORES
Clearance SALE
ON ALL
GROCERY MERCHANDISE
EVERYTHING
MUST GO
20% OFF
Clearance SALE
ON ALL
GROCERY MERCHANDISE
20% OFF

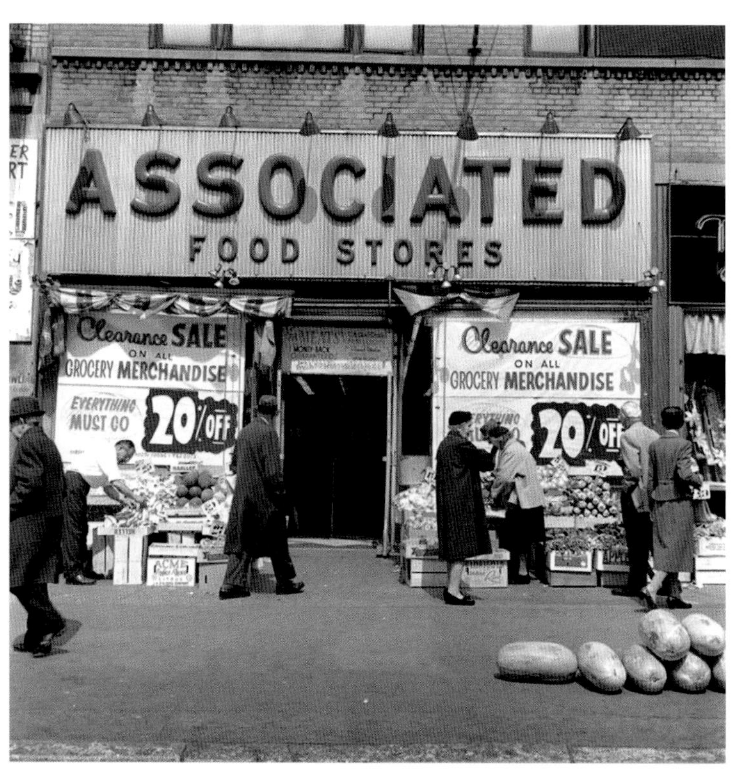

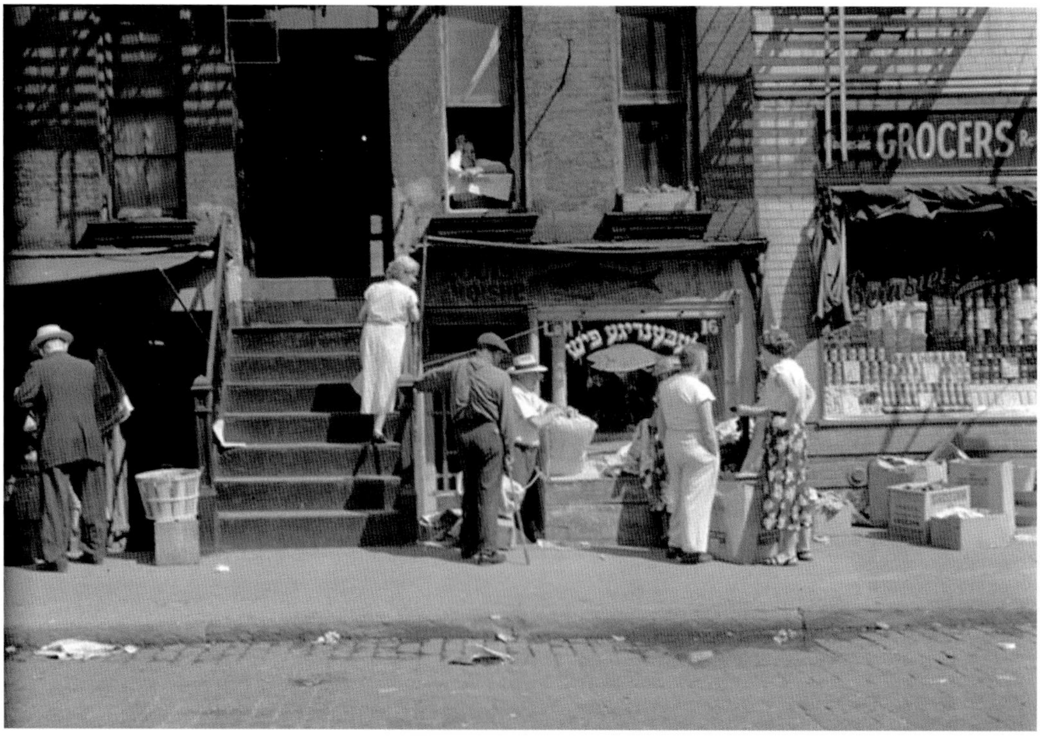
GROCERS

Taken for the *New York World-Telegram and the Sun Newspaper* in 1940, this photograph depicts a pushcart vendor, possibly Al Rabinowitz. As he places a bunch of grapes in a paper bag, he is clearly proud of the fruit and vegetables at his produce stand. [*Library of Congress*]

Opposite page:

Above: Pedestrians are strolling by an Associated Food Store in New York City. Juicy watermelons are laid out on the sidewalk and grocers are arranging fresh produce for a clearance sale. This moment was captured by photographer Morris Huberland around 1940. [*NYHM*]

Below: This photograph of people gathering around a grocery on a New York street was taken by Morris Huberland in the 1940s. The location is unknown, but it was a typical neighborhood in the city in those years of depression, war, and recovery. [*NYHM*]

Benny Brodsky, an animated pushcart vendor, is hard at work at his market stand in New York City. Given Benny's lively nature, it seems appropriate that the guy specialized in homemade pickles and horseradish. The photograph was taken in 1940 for the *New York World-Telegram and the Sun Newspaper*. [*Library of Congress*]

In July 1942, Howard Liberman photographed Charles Ruggiero, a grocer in an Italian neighborhood, wishing the fistful of spaghetti he is breaking was Mussolini's neck. The ceiling prices in Italian behind him helped in the defeat of the dictator by controlling inflation at home. [*Library of Congress*]

When Howard Liberman took his photograph in July 1942, Spiros Margrite and his Greek customers were well acquainted with the ceiling prices in his grocery—printed in Greek. By managing costs, Margarite helped destroy the fascists in his home country. [*Library of Congress*]

In August 1942, Marjory Collins photographed these Chinese men, probably the owners and operators in this grocery. The men posed, calm and composed, in their store in the bustling Chinatown of New York City in Lower Manhattan. [*Library of Congress*]

In August 1942, Marjory Collins photographed this storekeeper quickly adding up prices—income and expenses—on an abacus. The man is standing behind the counter in his grocery store in Chinatown, New York City. [*Library of Congress*]

In October 1942 Marjory Collins photographed this Czech doctor, his wife, Mrs. Winn [or Wynn], and their two daughters shopping for groceries in a corner market in New York. They are most likely refugees from the war. [*Library of Congress*]

FOOD STAMPS
REDEEMED HERE
FARMERS OF AMERICA
MOVE SURPLUS FOODS
SPHINX
BLACK FIGS
PYRAMID
CALIFORNIA
LILY
CALIFORNIA
WHITE FIGS

Marjory Collins photographed the customers and clerk in a grocery store on Mulberry Street in January 1943. This market was situated in a neighborhood in which Italian, Jewish, and Chinese people all made their homes. [*Library of Congress*]

Opposite page:

Above: Marjory Collins photographed this Italian meat stall in the First Avenue market at Tenth Street, New York City, in January 1943. Cuts of meat don't get any more varied and fresher than what was offered at this stall on this day. [*Library of Congress*]

Below: These three men were working in the Italian grocery in the First Avenue market at Tenth Street in New York City when Marjory Collin took this photograph in January 1943. It appears that the market is well-stocked, including many items from the Old Country. [*Library of Congress*]

While walking his beat, this Italian-American policeman chatted with the good-natured customers and owner in a grocery store on Mulberry Street in New York City. Marjory Collins took this candid photograph in the midst of World War II in January 1943. [*Library of Congress*]

Opposite page:

Above: In January 1943, Marjory Collins photographed Italian-American customers in a grocery on Mulberry Street, including a sailor who looks far too young to be fighting in a World War. The woman says she wished her son stationed overseas could see the photo of her. [*Library of Congress*]

Below: An Italian-American policeman chats with friends and neighbors in a grocery on Mulberry Street in New York City. The crowd appears cheerful and eager to bolster the spirit of others during the war. Marjory Collins took this photograph in January 1943. [*Library of Congress*]

Marjory Collins photographed the Jewish owner of this small grocery store on Mulberry Street in New York City in January 1943. The man is understandably proud of his bustling enterprise, and warmly welcomes every customer who walks into his store. [*Library of Congress*]

10

FULTON MARKET

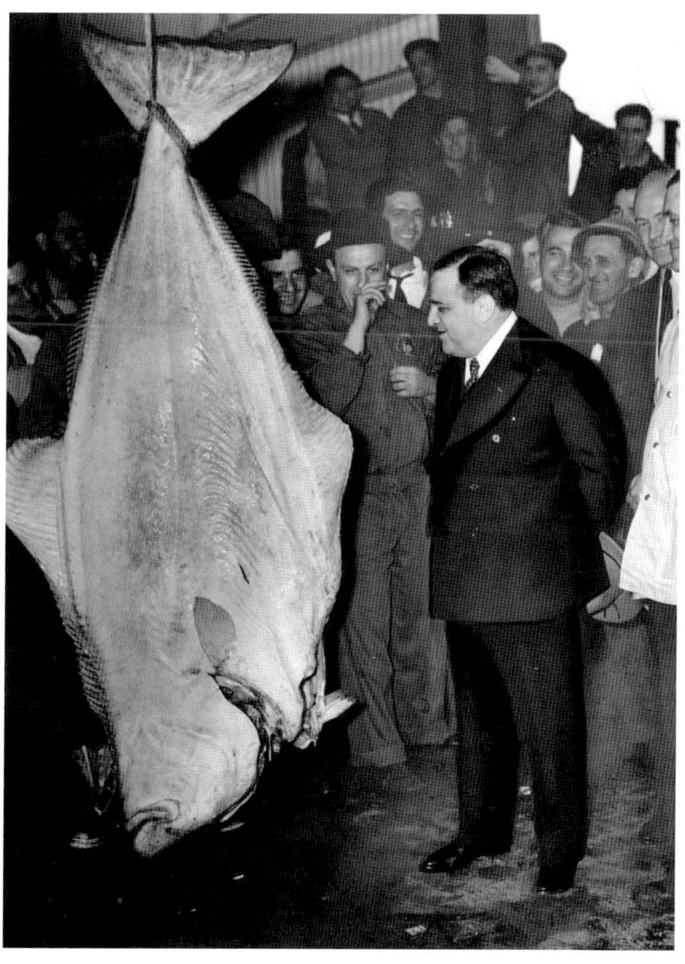

Mayor Fiorello Henry La Guardia poses with a 300-pound halibut at the Fulton Market in 1939. He appears upstaged by the fish, but what politician can resist a photo op? C. M. Stieglitz took this photo for the *New York World-Telegram and the Sun Newspaper*. [*Library of Congress*]

Amid the rigging, stevedores unload the day's catch from fishing boats at the Fulton Market onto the pier, or wharf, at Hunts Point in the Bronx, New York. Edward Lynch took this photograph for the *New York World-Telegram and the Sun Newspaper* in 1939. [*Library of Congress*]

Dock worker Buck Steo weighs another load of fresh mackerel at the Fulton Fish Market in Hunts Point in the Bronx, New York. Fred Palumbo took this photograph for the *New York World-Telegram and the Sun Newspaper* in 1939. [*Library of Congress*]

Gordon Parks photographed this dock worker at Fulton Market silhouetted against skyscrapers in May or June of 1943. The man is hard at work, bending over crates of iced-down fish to be delivered to fish stores and groceries throughout New York City. [*Library of Congress*]

In May 1943, Gordon Parks photographed this fruit vendor with his pushcart of fruits at the Fulton fish market New York City. The man struck a pose as he stood next to his pushcart with skyscrapers rising behind him. [*Library of Congress*]

Gordon Parks photographed this wholesaler's delivery truck being loaded with barrels of fish on the docks at the Fulton Fish Market in May or June of 1943. The fish will be delivered to groceries and fish markets throughout the New York metropolitan area. [*Library of Congress*]

Opposite page:

Above: Noted photographer Gordon Parks captured this moment on the dock at the Fulton Fish Market in May or June of 1943. These two sturdy workers are pushing up their tall, two-wheeled carts back to pick up more barrels or crates of fish caught that day. [*Library of Congress*]

Below: When Gordon Parks took this photograph in May or June of 1943, some wholesalers were still distributing fish throughout the city with horse-drawn wagons from Fulton Fish Market. Crates of iced-down fish are stacked high in this wagon. [*Library of Congress*]

Left: Mrs. Elizabeth Michelin is packing haddock fillets at the Jim Walsh Fillet Company at the Fulton Fish Market in 1943. Fred Palumbo photographed her hard at work for the *New York World-Telegram and the Sun Newspaper.* [*Library of Congress*]

Below: This glimpse inside the Fulton Fish Market shows an array of equipment—scales, crates, and baskets for sorting and icing down the fish caught that day. Walter Albertin took this photograph for the *New York World-Telegram and the Sun Newspaper* in 1954. [*Library of Congress*]

An unidentified man is weighing fish on a scoop scale at the Fulton Fish Market in 1963. As he was carefully checking the weight of each fish, Dick De Marsico photographed him for the *New York World-Telegram and the Sun Newspaper*. [*Library of Congress*]

These workers at the Fulton Fish Market are taking a break to warm themselves by a fire on a cold and windy March day in 1964. John Bottega took this candid group portrait for the *New York World-Telegram and the Sun Newspaper*. [*Library of Congress*]

11

NYC: FAMILIAR STREETS AND NEIGHBORHOODS

With a half-smoked stogie in his left hand, this fish merchant in the First Avenue market at Tenth Street stands proudly over that day's catch. Marjory Collins took his portrait as a character study in January 1943. [*Library of Congress*]

This street peddler has parked his pushcart loaded with string beans in along a street in Harlem, New York. He was carefully arranging the pile of string beans when the acclaimed Gordon Parks came by in May-June 1943 and took this fine photograph. [*Library of Congress*]

When they had a nickel or two, children promptly spent it at the candy counter in the grocery down the street. Other times they escaped the heat of summer on the East Side by splashing in an open fire hydrant. Roger Smith took this photograph in June 1943. [*Library of Congress*]

HOT JUMBO PEANUTS
TURKISH HALVAH
INDIAN NUTS 10
SUGARD PEANUTS 10
PLAIN RAISIN
POLICE DEPT
BUS STOP
NO PARKING

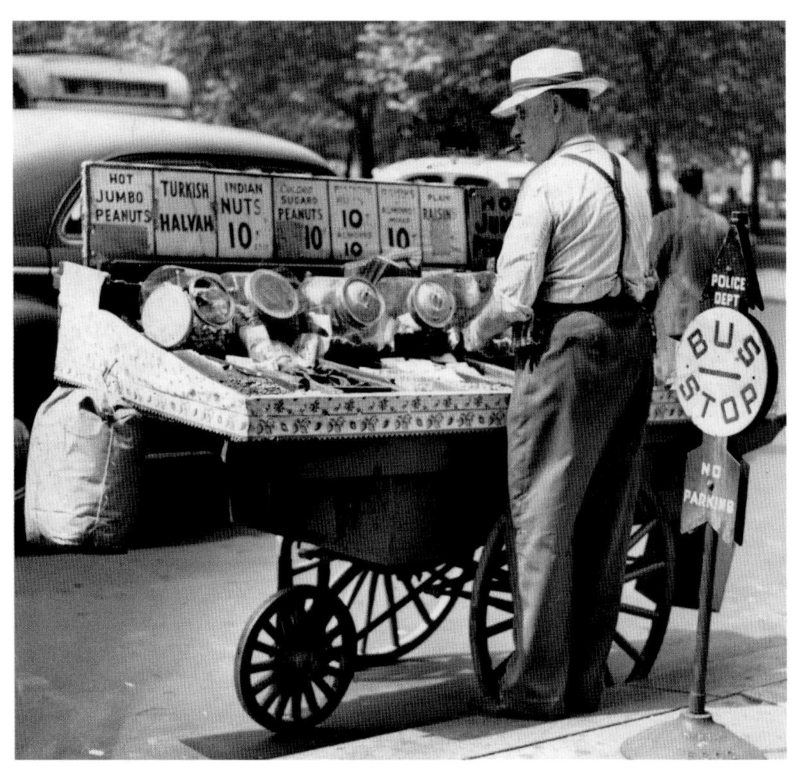

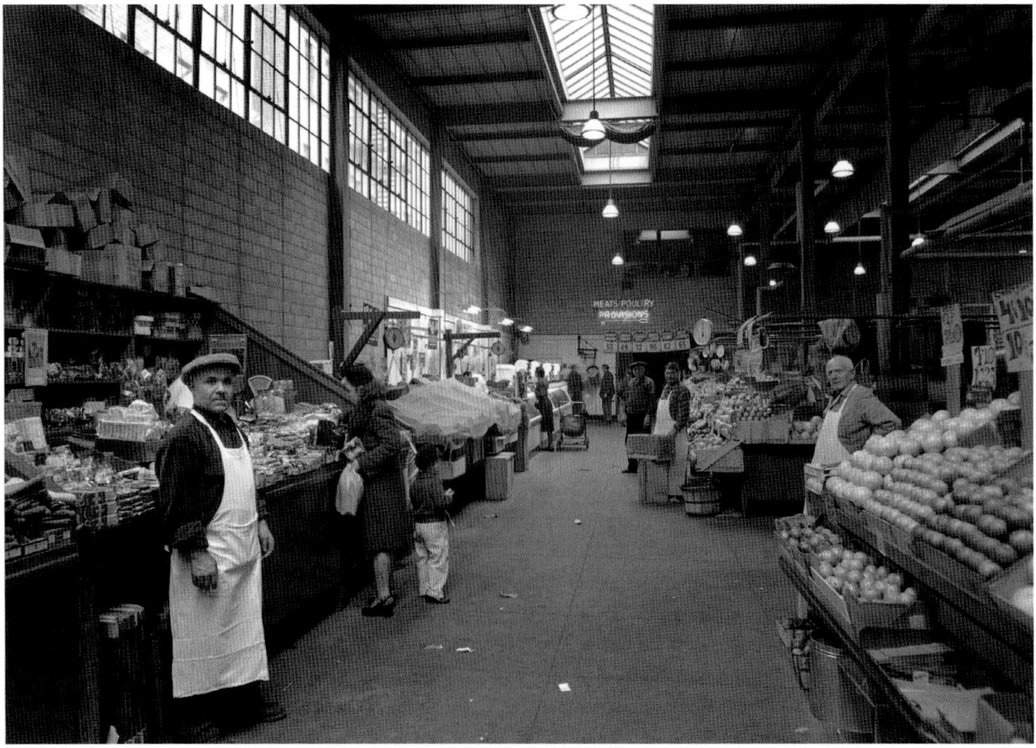
MEATS POULTRY
PROVISIONS

Pushcarts lined the street at the pushcart market on Belmont Avenue, 1960 Brooklyn, New York, when Roger Higgins took this photograph for the *New York World-Telegram and the Sun Newspaper* in 1960. [*Library of Congress*]

Opposite page:

Above: This street vendor is selling a variety of nuts from his pushcart at a bus-stop in an unknown location in New York City. Fred Palumbo took his photograph for the *New York World-Telegram and the Sun Newspaper* in 1947. [*Library of Congress*]

Below: On March 22, 1948, Gottscho-Schleisner, Inc. photographed the interior of the New York City Public Market, 1st Avenue and 73rd Street in New York City. Customers carefully look over the produce and clerks stand ready to assist them. [*Library of Congress*]

This overhead view of a pushcart at the curbside market on Belmont Avenue in Brooklyn illustrates the variety of fresh produce at these moving markets. Alan Fisher took the photograph for the *New York World-Telegram and the Sun Newspaper* in 1962. [*Library of Congress*]

Opposite page:

Above: This enterprise at the Brownsville market, Belmont Avenue, Brooklyn, New York City, looks like a general store on wheels. It was photographed by Roger Higgins for the *New York World-Telegram and the Sun Newspaper* in 1962, just before the bustling market closed. [*Library of Congress*]

Below: This street vendor was bundled up against the cold when he was photographed by Roger Higgins for the *New York World-Telegram and the Sun Newspaper* in 1962. The older man is sitting on a bushel basket by his pushcart of produce in Brooklyn, New York. [*Library of Congress*]

Ms. Ellen Lewin beams in the morning light as she shops at the Bleecker Street Market in 1962. She is standing in front of a scale along with crates and boxes of vegetables and fruit. Fred Palumbo photographed her for the *New York World-Telegram and the Sun Newspaper*. [*Library of Congress*]

This pushcart vendor is selling produce at the Belmont Avenue market in Brooklyn. Photographed by Roger Higgins for the *New York World-Telegram and the Sun Newspaper* in 1962, it appears that he is selecting the finest vegetables for one of his customers. [*Library of Congress*]

In 1962 Albert Pacetta, City Markets Commissioner, stood amid the pushcarts to announce the closing of this market at Saratoga Avenue and Prospect Place in Brooklyn. Roger Higgins captured the poignant moment for the *New York World-Telegram and the Sun Newspaper*. [*Library of Congress*]

Albert Pacetta, City Markets Commissioner, visited with Mollie Zeidman by her pushcart. It appears to be a special moment for Ms. Zeidman. Orlando Fernandez took her photograph for the *New York World-Telegram and the Sun Newspaper* in 1964. [*Library of Congress*]

Taken for *News Voice International* (New York, NY) in the 1960s, this vibrant photograph shows African-American families coming together at Park Avenue Market in East Harlem, Bronx, New York. [*Library of Congress*]

Photographed by Virginia B. Price for the Historic American Buildings Survey after 1933, this skyline depicts the South Street seaport area. Today, the neighborhood is largely comprised of Fulton Fish Market and the South Street Seaport Museum. But in the first half of the nineteenth century, the area became the mercantile center of the city and state, bustling with wholesale stores, warehouses, and counting houses. Merchants bought and sold imports and exports transported by ship to and from the East River harbor—and New York became the great city and state that it is today.